Tom Turner grew up in rural Ohio, leaving as a young man to attend West Point. After military service, he spent many years working in corporate America in senior management positions. He has been married for nearly 50 years, with three children and three grandchildren, and has lived in North Carolina for almost 40 years. He likes golf, writing, selling real estate, and date nights with his wife.

Dedicated to CT, Brad, Andrea, Sage, Grace, Dylan, Lilly Kate, Savannah, and all the friends who created this journey.

These poems are my story, pieces of me ripped out and put on paper to be my semi-real-life biography.

Tom Turner

The Coming of the Train

AUSTIN MACAULEY PUBLISHERS™

LONDON * CAMBRIDGE * NEW YORK * SHARJAH

Ordering Information
Quantity sales: Special discounts are available on quantity purchases by corporations, associations, and others. For details, contact the publisher at the address below.

Publisher's Cataloging-in-Publication data
Turner, Tom
The Coming of the Train

ISBN 9798889105794 (Paperback)
ISBN 9798889105800 (ePub e-book)

Library of Congress Control Number: 2023921463

www.austinmacauley.com/us

First Published 2024
Austin Macauley Publishers LLC
40 Wall Street, 33rd Floor, Suite 3302
New York, NY 10005
USA

mail-usa@austinmacauley.com
+1 (646) 5125767

Illustrations by Chloe Pouteau, who was extremely helpful in taking minimal artistic direction and creating illustrations that fit the needs of every poem for which she did an illustration.

Table of Contents

Preface

Life is a story told in hundreds of moments of laughter, pain, joy, and love –
experiences that wrap together and create a person, with all the resident emotions
that evolve from simply living.

My story is as random as everyone's – a myriad of puzzle pieces that only
occasionally truly fit together, and paint only a glimpse into the complexities that
are the human part of each of us.

This book is semi-autobiographical – partly word pictures that stroll through
periods of my life, and then it is often random thoughts or images from momentary
observations of daily life events. All of them are pages from the notes inside a
random mind.

I tried to gather my thoughts in chapters that had some continuity, which only
made me realize that only fragments of your life have continuity. Certainly, our
experiences growing up have a continuum, and falling in love could be semi-
charted – Beginnings of looking, losing (maybe several times), and finally finding
that right one.

But most of the rest of our lives are much more random. No one knows how
long a chapter might be, or when one chapter ends and another begins. No one
anticipates tragedy or facing death – man lives on hope, and not on planning for
the worst – but tragedy and facing survival changes a lot of perspectives. And
sometimes, thoughts are just too random to fit in any specific place.

Even when life semi-sorts itself out, when right people happen, when some
stability seems to impose itself, random events and thoughts and moments still
find time to sneak in through the cracks, to remind you that no matter what we
believe, life is a collection of random moments.

The Coming of the Train

There is only
Hello
then
In Between
and then
Goodbye

The Coming of the Train

One day an old and worn-out train
will come along and call my name,
and I will know to climb inside.

There'll be no reason for me to run.
I'll have no shadow in the sun
and know there is no need to hide.

And then the man I tried to be
will look out the glass and see
fields of dreams and azure skies.

And I will have no fears or tears
and will not pray for one more day.

The train runs swiftly on silent tracks
and my yesterdays will be flash backs,
thousands in the blink of an eye.

Wave to me, and do not cry
as the whistle blows and I pass by
on one last ride to see the sea.

And then the man I tried to be
will look out across that sea,
and see horizons of goodbye.

And I will have no fears or tears
and will not pray for one more day.

A Blank Piece of Paper

Everyone starts out as a child
with a blank piece of paper,
a box of crayons,
an imagination,
and no doubts.

And then adults tell them
to color inside the lines,
what color a flower should be,
how tall a tree grows, and
use a new piece of paper.

I always wondered what was wrong
with my sorta square brown flowers,
and trees too tall for airplanes.
And why no one ever told me
those are great just the way they are.

Maybe that's why, in my later years
I picked up my paper and crayons again,
and began to write with words,
the pictures I always wanted to paint

Alfred

She named him Alfred.
The tree where we would park
and talk about dreams
or climb in the back seat
and create our passion scenes.

Back in the days
when people parked
instead of tweeted,
and loved instead of liked.

Flying with Wings on Fire

We were fast cars, back road racing,
kids with no missions
except the next good time
around the next curve or corner,
flying with wings on fire.

We were a small-town road show,
fast friends sharing life at 3-digit speeds,
and that wild man wild times bullet-proof
young man kind of life,
just flying with wings on fire.

Eating life like a buffet
of crazy endless days
and never-ending roads,
daredevils laughing at it all,
just flying with wings on fire.

And then one day we watched
as they put out your fire
and folded your wings,
too young to be
flying no more.

Leaving Ohio

Leaving that farm town seemed so easy,
driving past knee-high corn fields
and browning wheat fields,
suitcase in back, airport ahead.

I didn't realize it then, but I'd never return
to the city park and horseshoe pits,
back road racing and back road parking,
and local spots only the boys all knew.

In our story-telling nights, the girls
were always wilder than our truth,
but boys must be boys before
they grow out from youth.

And so, the hot rod cars and
green football jerseys and
late-night skinny-dipping world
quietly was laid to rest.

We all go back, but only to visit.
The past is just a photograph
of what was, never to be again,
pictures of what can never change.

The pages turn, the chapters close.
The years of youth, like us, disappear
in the perpetual motion of the clock,
never to return.

The Great Mythunderstanding

I'm not sure how it happened.
I'm really not sure why.
I thought she was saying goodnight.
But she was saying goodbye.

Katidid

Late at night
I hear the katydids
in the field and
around the pond
behind the house,
reminding me that
Katidid
said she loved me.

She said she did.
She said it,
and now
I do not know
if it is better
to believe she did
and wonder why
she quit
or to believe
Katidid only said it.

The Glow in the Dark Bar
and Sidewalk Cafe

I walk down to the park
to The Glow In The Dark
Bar and Sidewalk Café,
to my space
away from you place.

I'll think about
what we were
when we were
better than
what we are.

I'll look around at the
concrete skies and neon stars,
and I'll get drunk enough
to let go of my dreams
again, for one more night.

The Moment

The silence is louder
than any cannon
in the moment
before battle begins.

I crouch, waiting,
scared, angry,
ready to kill
the man across the field
who is my enemy.

And in the moment
before battle begins,
I realize
that I am also
the man across the field.

I am millions
of men across the fields
in thousands of battles
through thousands of years,
waiting
in the moment
before battle begins.

Wild Ride

We'd been at church all Friday night,
drinking the holy water.
And on the way to somewhere else
we stopped to buy more blessed stuff.

A case of beer, I said,
and I will ride my bike
from here to there
across the railing of this bridge.
A dark steel flowing arch,
at least 10 inches wide
would take me on my midnight ride
over the river to the other side.

My headlight pierced the moonless night
as up the rail I rode. I yell
You will all owe me –
and then – OH HELL!

On the down side of that steel belt
the light shone out into only darkness,
and not onto my narrow path.
The tire slipped off the edge – and FELL

Hanging on the bridge, I watched
that 40-foot slow motion trip
and cried out #&%!#@&%$
when I heard it hit.

My bike in pieces
on the rocks below,
the remains a remainder
of a drunken ego.

Marbles in a Box

Everyone gets a box
of marbles in their life.
Shooters by the score.

And every day we pull one out
And shoot it at the world.

Sometimes you move the world,
sometimes it swallows you up.

But tomorrow you always get
another marble.

The World Is Ending

The world is coming to an end –

it's gloom and doom again.
But I don't pay attention to the signs –
my world has ended many times.

Somehow, sometime next week,
or even tomorrow morning,
or just one day
without me knowing,
it begins all over again.

Dares

I dare say, we all should have
said no to the Bad Idea Fairy
and passed a few times
on those dares we've taken.

But then again, no one
looks back on their life
and reminisces about the nights
of long and restful sleep.

But sometimes I still wonder about
waking face-planted that morning,
in the grass skirt, cowboy boots,
ZZ Top t-shirt, and earring.

Where the hell did I get them?
Why was I wearing them?
Who's were they?

AND WERE THERE ANY PICTURES?

Why?

Why do people feel the need
to pull you back
when you want to fly?

To check off boxes
that define what you
must be and try?

To create a list of what you
cannot be and draw boundaries
that try to limit you more?

To tell you all the dangers
if you fail, instead of
the glory if you soar?

Life Is Just A...

cake mix that never sees the oven.
Every day we add
a few more ingredients,
trying to make the recipe great.
And in the end, we hope
it's not sent to Hell to bake.

2 Rows of 3

Another one in 2 rows
marches to the drumstick click.
2 rows of 3
carry one more soldier home.

A mother cries, maybe a wife,
listen to the drumstick click,
2 rows of 3
carry one more soldier home.

The young are pawns
and pay the price
of leaders in chambers
safely at home.

And so another, and another,
marches to the drumstick click.
2 rows of 3
carry one more soldier home.

Seasons of a Life

The early spring is barely a memory,
sneaking in on toddler toes until
old enough to be fresh-legged
running basepaths, learning to flirt,
and hoping to win. At everything.

Summer should be the best season,
but seldom was, because
there was always too much heat from
bills to pay and work to finish
and endless juggling of the hours.

Autumn seems to be the gentlest time,
as hair turns gray like leaves turn orange,
in days of softer suns and longer shadows,
when rivers flow more slowly, patiently
just waiting for tomorrows.

Winter winds are stronger now, and colder.
But I made it to here, to that time of life
when clocks move faster,
and hours are shorter,
and days and nights seem fewer.

I have touched the boundaries
of all the days of every season,
and do not regret a single one.
Soon the sun will be going down.
It always does, you know.

The Year of All Dark Days

The 3 O'clock News

11 October 1971

It's not your back
they said.
The problem's
in your head.

A lump,
they said,
unreachable
untreatable.

There's nothing we can do
they said
under the knife
to save your life.

Future Goodbye, Future

The doctors tell me that
the headaches will get stronger
and the back and legs will not,
until I cannot stand or sit or walk.

I came back home,
but not to live a lie.
And everyone soon will know
I'm only here for a long goodbye.

I can't tell my friends and parents' yet,
I wish I could tell them all.
But I don't want the grieving
before grieving becomes real.

Most of all, there's one
who deserved the truth
I couldn't give her.
A real goodbye, and not a lie.

I wish I could have told her
why I just walked away.
Angry and broken-hearted
is less than she deserved.

But I do not have the time
to love her anymore
I only have the time
to help her unlove me.

And I can bear the thought
of doing this alone, more than
watching pain in her eyes,
watching me go.

Knowing she will heal from
a broken heart and life for her
will go on much sooner,
and that she does deserve.

A Gathering of Forces

The rain is softer now –
has been for a day or so,
waiting for a break
or a gathering of forces.

This is not the first time
this storm has eased,
and so I wait, weary,
leery
because the storm cloud still remains.

I think more in lulls,
more hopeful of the end,
more fearful
of a gathering of forces

Driftwood

Lying here, in the sand,
under unseen stars
blanked by rain clouds,
amidst seaweed and sand crabs,
and broken shells.

I am a piece of driftwood
tossed on the shore
by waves of a world
that cares not where I land,
or whether or not
I float back out to sea.

Nowhere Road

Been holding on, doing ok,
kinda, some days.
Not really though –
just what I say

I keep moving on,
running through the night,
down this nowhere road
with no guiding light

Tired of feeling
like just getting by
and losing hope
at the speed of life.

Last Leaves

Bourbon and pills and cigarettes
and midnight motorcycle rides
never help, never numb
the mind enough to all the pain.

No need to count the hours or days –
there are too few, to be wasted
by moments contemplating
might have beens and what remains.

My last few leaves are clinging to my tree,
life's winter wind is soon to be
blowing down my neck, hinting at
maybe one more spring.

I believe it's worse,
knowing.
Better to fall off a horse or
have your parachute not open

Christmas Solitude

Sitting, looking out the window,
only me and darkness
waiting on the Christmas sun.

Wondering what is next to do –
sun doesn't fix the solitude.
Maybe I will just go out and run.

Run forever, until I find
the mystery edge of earth,
keep running 'til I'm gone.

The Tide

The March deadness
blows down the beach.
I sit. Without the nerve
to walk on, but with nerve enough
not to walk away.

Water at my feet.
Tired.
I will not run-walk away.
The tide is slowly coming in.

Dark Days

If there were some way,
if I could find it,
I would leave this body behind.

Undress completely
from my bones
and leave my flesh.

I would be silence,
void of any thought,
totally absent of me.

I would forget
my breath
and all my sounds.

I would walk on hands
in fear of footprints,
tracks of a five-toed bird.

I would become an absence
of words, thoughts, memories:
a five-toed bird taken to flight.

And in the year
of all dark days
I would be forgotten.

We Are All

Another grain of sand
on a summer beach
waiting on a midnight tide.

Another leaf
on an autumn tree
waiting on a winter wind.

Another flake of snow
in a winter storm
waiting on a warmer sun.

Another drop of rain
in a spring shower
waiting to evaporate.

We are all just waiting
for whatever takes us
forever away.

For Me in May

I've given up praying
for things I want.
I still believe
there is a God,
I've just quit asking Him
for things for me.
They are, after all,
not things I need.

I have no dog or friend
wife or child
to be taken care of
when He decides
it's time I meet Him
face to face.

So I have no need
for things to leave behind.

Sand Dollar

I am a sand dollar
you find on the beach.
once beautiful, now broken.
Pick me up and skip me
back out to the sea.
And just let me die me.

Rain

I am dancing naked in the rain.
There is no better way to dance.
And nowhere else to dance.
But in the rain.

I do not dodge the drops.
I do not try as I once did.
There is nothing else to do but dance.
And in the rain.

I did not really dance before,
although I really thought I did.
Before I learned nothing is stronger
than the rain.

And I wore clothes, back then
when I really thought I danced.
Before I learned the need for nothing
in the rain.

I am dancing naked in the rain.
It's doing its work, beating me down
until there is no one remaining.
Just the rain.

Against the Current

Swimming against the current
on this river road of life,
pushed further away
from ever reaching home.
Never giving up
but drowning in the fight.

Roll the Dice

11 July 1972

You have about 100 days.
Plus a few or
minus a few,
that's all you get.
Some good, some bad
Until they end.

So maybe test the odds?
With some method new, unproven.
Lose, and you get 10 days or less.
Win, and maybe get
a chance at life?

Screw the odds.
Roll the dice.

Guinea Pigs

14 October 1972

When hope seems gone
and days seem dark
I drop to one knee
and think of 23.

Fifteen and me,
the untreatables,
agreed to be
guinea pigs
for experimental surgery.

One by one,
we dropped, to 10,
then 6, then 3
then only me.

Sometimes I question why
I was the one to survive
But mostly I thank God
I am one alive.

Traveler

Traveler

Watch for me.
I slip by easily,
a breath of wind
on April nights.

Watch for signs of me
in the road
to know that I have been –
dust, disturbed
by feet shuffled restlessly
in places I have paused too long.

And if you look to find me,
do not look where I have been,
for I do not return.

Man-Shell

Sometimes late at night
I become a man-shell
sitting there,
not sad,
not happy,
not anything.

Not thinking
about tomorrows or dreams
or anything

It's just me
and walls, and random noise.
Nothing else.

Just me
waiting
and waiting.

The Heart Is a Hawk

Perched, waiting
Silently watching, ready.
The heart is always looking
for signs in the forest.
A soft word,
a gentle touch,
a smile or tear,
are all the heart needs
to believe a chance is near.

Sailboat

I am just a sailboat
sitting on a calm sea
bobbing up and down
on the waves,
but just drifting.

My flag is hoisted,
my sails are furled,
but no wind blows.
I am just waiting
for someone to be my wind.

Someone Somewhere

Hey! Someone somewhere!
It's me, over here.
Another someone somewhere
looking too.

Looking everywhere,
both ways at every corner,
for someone somewhere,
lurking, searching too.

Yo-Yo

Up and down, up and down.
Find someone, lose someone.
Find again, lose again.
Try again, try again, try again

It's not a battle, or a war,
but every encounter leaves a scar.

Cowboy

I've always been a cowboy,
saddled up,
ready for love at first sight
with every cowgirl
who rode in from the night.

I've always been a cowboy,
always saddled up,
ready to ride off into the sunset
every time that cowgirl
got too close to being too right.

Escape

The eastern wind blows cold
as I settle down
on the Georgia beach
this November night.

The chill burrows deep
inside my coat
and the driftwood fire
struggles to keep me warm.

A few lights on fishing boats
blink as they lift and set
on bobbing waves,
like stars on cloudy nights.

A distant moon casts
a single lighted path
out from the shore
to darkness far away.

A sand crab crawls
across the tide-foam at my feet,
his everyday world
much simpler than mine.

The eastern wind blows cold
as I settle down to this escape,
but never as cold as that world of
concrete jungles and neon stars.

Road Lover

I am a lover of the road
because it has no fences,
no boundaries to contain
a rambling warrior of the heart.

The road leads to and from
anywhere and nowhere,
to chance moments in the sun
and the times to run.

I never meant to be the guy
to kiss and run,
playing heart roulette
with everyone.

But others on the road
do not seem to see
I am not here to stay,
I am a runner, free.

The road's my friend,
my only lover.
And when my world gets tough
there is always another.

Red Riding Hood

She is the wild one,
blazing eyes and flowing hair,
running crazy through her world.

The men all fall, one by one,
hearts tortured by their dreams
of the one untamable.

No one understands,
she is Red Riding Hood,
inviting in the wolf.

The Stranger

Highways all run to somewhere –
from a place you leave to a place you go.
Towns or cities or country bars
at one end to
towns or cities or country bars
at the other end.

And I will always be
the stranger passing through,
running highways from end to end.
Going to and from places
with no faces
that remember me.

Heart on Wheels

I tried my damnedest but
I'm just not the one to stay.
I'm not the one to settle down
I'll always be the one that got away.

I've got a heart on wheels,
packed and ready for flight,
running shoes by my bed
and car keys by the light.

There have been a few
who tried to hold me still.
But everyone who tries can see
I'm being held against my will.

No scuffs on my boot toes
from dragging on too long,
no tears running down my face
from loving you country songs.

I've got a heart on wheels,
packed and ready for flight,
running shoes by my bed
and car keys by the light.

Red Rover, Red Rover

We were strangers.
Then lovers.
Now strangers again.
Red Rover, Red Rover,
Send someone new over.

Pinata

Sometimes,
love dresses you up as a
Pinata
and lets everyone
beat you till you break.

Feelings

I let you in, knowing
you might break something.
Dishes
Doors
Hearts

I knew, but didn't understand
that feelings have a life cycle.
Grow
Pain
Die

And so, I let you in
and learned about
Joy
Anger
Tears

Mostly, I have learned
that feelings are just
Hello
Smile
Goodbye

Someone New

I live alone
in my four-corner world.
But sometimes at night
I'm not so sure I'm really here.

Once a week a maid comes in,
cleans the ashtrays
changes the bed
and makes the room smell new.

Nothing seems more barren then.
The smell of even me is gone,
leaving no trace of what I've been
last week, or if I even was.

Week to week someone new,
lost to who I was the week before,
lives in my room
and is my new me.

Week to week someone new
spends the nights
looking for the someone old
who lived here long ago.

Dance Partners

No one gets to choose
who hurts them in life's dance.
They only get to choose
who gets the chance.

Be careful of the partners
you pick to dance along.
Just because they dance with you
doesn't mean they hear your song.

Leak

I've had so many
cuts and stabs and
holes punched in me
by the women who
passed through my life,
that when a new one
comes along and
we drink a toast to us
I leak all over
everything we try to be.

Evolution

Everything evolves.
Species improve
or become extinct.
Mountains and oceans
grow and shrink.
Love
grows or goes.

Women Cause Drinking

Women are the #1
cause of drinking.

When you find the right one
and times are fun,
you drink to celebrate.

When the right one
becomes the wrong one,
you drink to forget.

And when there isn't one,
and you are hoping for one,
you drink to pass the time.

I Remember

In the darkest morning hours
I remember the best of times,
the best of nights with you.
I remember.

In the darkest morning hours
I remember you dancing and
you laughing at me dancing.
I remember.

In the darkest morning hours
I remember, smiles and tears,
hopes and dreams and fears.
I remember.

In the darkest morning hours
I remember me, raging
racing back, too late.
I remember

In the darkest morning hours
I remember.
I remember.

I Believe

I believe
in Santa Claus
Peter Pan
the Easter Bunny
and Love.
Although sometimes
I am not so sure
about the latter.

On My Way

This New York world is just too big;
the organ grinder never seems to stop.
I need to get back to your touch.
Just one more project to get done.
I was almost on my way to you, but
you were already on your way away,
you were already on your way gone.

Denver is just too cold for me;
I need the beach and summer sun.
A few more snowfalls and my
writing here will soon be done.
I was almost on my way to you, but
you were already on your way away,
you were already on your way gone.

Folly Beach just sounded right:
the perfect place to hide and finish
what I never seem to get completed.
Not much longer, I'll be home.
I was almost on my way to you, but
you were already on your way away,
you were already on your way gone.

Tough World

It becomes a tough world
when someone you know
becomes someone you used to know,
when someone you cared for
becomes someone who doesn't care
and somewhere you are
becomes somewhere you were.

Headlights in the Night

I grew up in Smalltown
dreaming of city lights.
I had songs to sing
and stories to write.
A boy going somewhere
behind headlights in the night.

Packed my guitar,
said my goodbyes.
A guy going somewhere
behind headlights in the night.

I wasn't 2 kids, a dog,
and a minivan man.
I was a man going somewhere
Behind headlights in the night.

Now my songs have all been sung.
Stories have all been told.
Just an old man going nowhere,
behind headlights in the night.

Bruises

There are some bruises
collected along the way
that I just never
talk about.

Words, said and unsaid.
Backs turned away.
Eyes, staring fiercely
or just turned down

People sometimes leave a mark –
probably never knowing
they put a dent in some
unsuspecting heart.

I would guess
I've left some too.

Guest Book

People in your life
are just visitors –
signing into your guest book
while passing through
for a minute or two,
a day or two,
a year or two.

We are all just visitors
in everyone's guest books,
sometimes caring,
sometimes sharing
a dream or two
before passing through,
to the next guest room
and the next new visitor.

Life is just chalk drawings
on the sidewalk,
worn away by traffic
or washed away by tears,
fading away like the names
in your guest book.

Shake my hand,
sign my book,
say goodbye.

Wandering Through
Mind Fields

Wandering Through Mind Fields

I always thought one day
I'd have it figured out,
how to quiet the wandering mind,
drifting recklessly through airstream fields,
meandering along mental highways
going somewhere – or nowhere –
a runner with feet on fire
running through lava rocks.

I always thought one day
I'd have it figured out,
but I am still wandering through mind fields,
rambling past pain and pleasure
and time-out playgrounds,
with strangely random thoughts,
never where I meant to be, but
always hoping I'm on my way.

Midnight BB's

Midnights on the porch.
drink in one hand,
cigarette in the other,
with a pad of paper
and a pen for when
some crazy musing
comes to mind –
a BB bouncing in the brain,
sometimes bursting out
and finding its way onto some
soon-to-be forgotten note.

Random Mind

Sometimes I feel the pieces of me
are no more than
socks and underwear,
randomly stuffed in a drawer,
symbols of the pieces of a mind
stuffed not so neatly in a man.

Today I'll put on yellow socks,
blue pants and green striped shirt,
red baseball cap with
Batman tennis shoes,
and other random choices.

And everyone who sees me knows
my mind works randomly like my clothes.

I Strongly Dislike

I strongly dislike
People who hate.
because of color
or where they lived
or who they love
or even their favorite team.

I strongly dislike
People who judge.
as if they know 'right'
better than you.
I leave all that
For God to do.

Do Not Judge

When you meet a politician,
do not judge too quickly.
Remember,
once upon a time,
they were human too
and had a heart and soul.

Red Stop Sign

A black man and
A blond man and
A brown man
all sat down to dinner.
And no one noticed.
Isn't that the way
It's meant to be?

Why can't we be
Black or
Blond or
Brown,
with no meaning,
after all.

Why do we
make it more
than a red stop sign
or golden arches?

Vegetarians

Seems to me, if God
wanted us to be vegetarians,
he would have had Noah
build a smaller Ark
and just take 2 of every seed.

Random Wisdom #124

Man is supposed to be
the most intelligent form
of life on the planet.

Yet only man puts
tattoos on his face
and drugs in his veins
and jumps off bridges.
Only man has to be convinced
that life is worth a fight.
Only man gives up.

Even a cricket will
fight to stay alive.

The Path

The path through the woods
seems to entice the eye.
The solitude is clamoring,
calling, screaming, that I
should follow it
to that quiet place
where I can dream
in solitary space.

Hoping on the End of a Rope

Sometimes we need to just let go –
We can't forever be the man
hoping on the end of a rope
dangling over the river.

There is a need to let go –
people, memories, things.
Drop into the river.
Life doesn't just stop.

Eye of the Hurricane

Sometimes it's just better
to quietly allow
your enemies to underestimate
your strengths and your resolve.

Let them forget
how quiet the wind becomes,
in the eye of the hurricane.

It's Hell Being Black

It's hell being black –
No one talks to you.
And they all think
You're dangerous too.

So I bought a blue coat
To cover my black.
And no one shuns me
In my blue sack.

Now the world seems fine
As I pretend to be
One of you, but
Why can't I just be me?

The Shell

The shell of the gun
left the shell of a man.
Twice.
The one shot and killed and
the one who shot and killed.

Cake

In six days, God created
earth and man,
and on the seventh day
He rested.

But on the eighth
He realized
His work was incomplete,
and He created
chocolate cake.

Albatross

It seemed that day as if
the world had finally
found its way.
Hand-in-hand
along the beach
sailboats on the water
and sea gulls in the air,
picking scraps up off the beach.
The day ended so softly.
But the ship sails out the harbor.
And the albatross is gone.

It seemed that night crept in
to find the world
had lost its way.
Hands-in-pockets
moonlight on the water
walking alone, kicking
seashells on the beach,
The day ended so swiftly.
But the ship sails out the harbor.
And the albatross is gone.

Jenga

Why do so many people
treat love like a giant
game of Jenga
and start pulling
little pieces out
until it all just
crashes down?

HPM2

We are the homeless,
that faceless blob in tent cities,
under bridges, on park benches,
in doorways and the woods.

We are the homeless,
the ones without TV
to hear the lies about
for everyone and unity.

We are the homeless,
that's what you call us,
our name is just Homeless,
not John or Jane, or even people.

We don't vote and
we don't donate.
We don't burn and riot.
So our voices are never heard.

We are the homeless,
People, not just homeless
Homeless People Matter Too.
HPM2

Eagle Wings

Wish I could fly on eagle wings,
floating on the highest winds,
above the darkest days
and dismal memories.
I wish I could fly.

Wish I could soar on eagle wings,
drifting along on quiet winds,
safe from the damage
I've done below.
I wish I could fly.

Wish I could fly, wish I could fly,
high above my world,
waiting for pain to cease,
waiting for my peace,
Wish I could fly.

Dunce

I guess I'm not very smart,
maybe even a little stupid
or possibly even a complete dunce.
I keep trying to do this foolish thing
called thinking on my own.

I'm probably not very good at
understanding data and information,
concepts and theories, and
using logic and problem solving,
to form opinions of my own.

So I guess I should just keep trusting
NBC
CBS
ABC
FOX
CNBC
Facebook
Twitter
Politicians

Silence

Silence is the color
of the break of day
or the dark of night.
I do not mind being alone
in a room or woods, or
on a beach or street
with just silence.
Sometimes silence
has a lot to say.

The Raucous Liberal

I am the Raucous Liberal.
It is my right to protest.
Ardently and violently.
Not only <u>for</u> my beliefs
but also <u>against</u> yours.

Freedom of Speech
is mine, and only mine.
If you want to voice
an opinion that differs
I WILL shout you down,
shame you to silence,
boycott your business
and call you racist or
any other derogatory
name I choose.

I will hide behind
worthwhile causes
to create disruption
and destruction.

Freedom of speech
is mine – and only mine.
You have no right to
disagree with me.
So shut the hell up.

基督教育年会

This is YMCA in Chinese.
How do you dance to that?

The Best We Have

The best we have
dress in olive drab
or blue or white
and go to fight
and die forgotten
by those dressed
in politician suits,
with statues built
to honor them
for sending the best
to die and lie
beneath forgotten crosses.

Men, Just Wondering

If OK is OK
and Good is Good
and Great is Great,
why isn't Fine, Fine?

You Don't Have to Wait

You don't have to wait
until the heart heals
and the memories die
and the pain is gone.

You don't have to wait
until the hands work better
or the legs work better,
or the body is not sore.

You don't have to wait
until the mind sees clearly
or the eyes see without
tears to blur the sight.
You don't have to wait
until the road is certain,
and your companions
are the right ones.

You don't have to wait
until life doesn't hurt
to be happy.

Burning Bridges

Sometimes it's important
to burn some bridges along the way.
Sometimes the only way forward
is to lose the safe retreat.

The Lonely Shell

The lonely shell stood vigil
over her sad ocean.
Her mind's eyes crying,
watching her friend dying.

She needs protection –
species netted to extinction,
waters stained with pollution.
Someone stop this execution!

Junk washes up and
trash litters her shores.
Quote the raven,
My Shore – Nevermore!

The Odds

Death will come –

no one will beat the odds.
So why live life so cautiously,
that when it comes,
you regret the path you've taken.

Our lives are meant
to challenge all the odds,
to love and laugh and live
a life so full that
death is just a punctuation mark.

The Booth

At the corner of
Justice Way and MLK Drive
he set up a booth
under a light
and a sign that read
Right of Way

He put up a banner
over his booth –
Media Must Always
Tell The Truth.

The press rallied around
and tore the booth down
and shot out the light –
no one could tell them
the Way of Right.

Hear the Voices

I hear the voices, all the voices,
of those who've fallen,
that I might sing.

I hear the voices, all the voices,
singing "O Say Can See"
for those who'll never sing again.

I hear the voices, all the voices,
of those who died
that I might live, to sing free.

I hear the voices, all the voices,
of those who remain, singing
and praying for those gone.

One More Farmer No More

A farmer through and through –
he loved the fields and crops and dirt,
and that magic he could work.

He loved sunrise tractors in the fields
and cows in pastures,
and planting neat rows of corn and wheat.

But time marches on –
it spares not the good men –
and so, one day, he could not plow again.

And then the men in suits and cars
came in from the uptown bars
to bulldoze all the barns.

They sold all the animals
cut down the trees, cleared the fields,
and planted neat rows of solar panels.

Better or Different

We all live in this illusion
that life could have been
better or different,
if we'd just done something
better or different.
But it never could have been
better or different –
it happened, it is
and nothing can change it,
not any of it at all.

Reality is not
the might have been.

Dogs

I like all dogs –
And wish I could say the same
about people.
But people are more like cats.

The Beach

The beach is the truest portrait of life.
Waves are like the days of living,
sometimes washing ashore gently,
and sometimes crashing painfully.

Seashells are like old memories,
once vivid and beautiful,
now weathered and scattered
by the tides of time.

Tiny crabs come out at night,
looking for scraps of the day,
like memories searching for
better pieces of yesteryear.

Lives are the footprints in the sand,
Slowly filling with sand and ocean
and washed away
by the tides of time.

A Man Is Dying

I heard today
A man is dying.

I guess that's
insignificant
in this age
of atom bombs
Viet Nam
Kennedys and King
Iraq, Iran and
Afghanistan,
50,000 dead on roads,
thousands on Chicago streets
and 100,000 dead on opioids.

I mean,
he's just ONE man.
JUST one.
And what's just ONE MORE?

Those of you
who think this true
do not know
the man is you.

Pandas

Are Pandas
Black with White trim
or
White with Black trim?

Or are they just Bears
and black and white
are just colors.

No Matter What

No matter what you want to do,
the timing is always wrong,
conditions are all wrong,
the right people aren't along.

No matter what you want to do,
it will always be impossible,
until you realize
you only need to start.

The Last Beginning

The Last Beginning

You're a strange world
laughing eyes
softness,
tears for crushed flowers.

You make a strange world
out of me
when you touch me
and make think about
kids and kites
and going to church again
on Sundays
and breaking promises
I made to me.

Be a Light

040411

Be a candle
in the darkness.
Light a path.
Be a light.

Too much hate.
Too much spite.
Share your kindness
Be a light.

In the middle
of the fight,
be the peace.
Be a light.

There is no need
for always right
win every fight
words that bite
fears that incite
to prove your might.
The world needs help
just being alright.

Be a candle
in the night.
In the darkness
light a path.
Be a light.

McDonalds Men's Club

For Dad: 102312

They meet in the corner at McDonalds
every Wednesday.
Old men drinking coffee, talking softly
And every now and then
the club gets smaller again.

Everyone thinks it's just old men
with nothing to do.
Passing time and watching time passing.
But the manager knows why they come
and he gives them coffee free.

Together many years ago, they
Shot down two planes at Pearl Harbor
Landed at Omaha Beach
Survived the Bataan Death March
Won a Silver Star and two Purple Hearts
at the Battle of the Bulge
And freed Auschwitz.

Just old men sitting in the corner
at McDonalds.
Every Wednesday

Why God Made Women

After God made man, He realized
that man would need someone to
correct him when telling a story,
tell him how to drive,
help him with colors,
and remind him about his manners.

Also, to hold him in tough times,
cry with him when dreams die,
and celebrate when dreams fly.
Remind him to call his mother,
be his cheerleader and confidant,
and remind him to be human.

So Quickly

Thank you for dropping in –
I know our time is short.
So quickly you will…

Learn to tie a bow,
count to 10, and
catch a ball.

Make your own ponytail,
drive a car.
Flirt.

Find a guy.
Say goodbye.

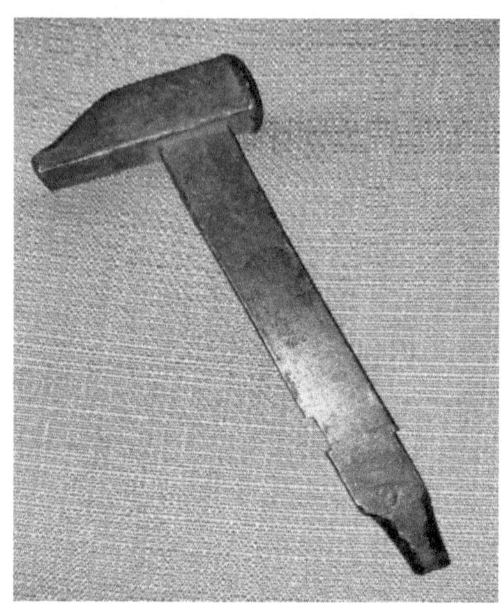

The Tool

I have this tool –
I don't know what it is.
My dad gave it to me,
and his dad gave it to him.
I've used it as a hammer
And used it as a punch.
It works well as a lever
and also as a wedge.
One day I too will pass it down.
And like my dad did to me,
let everyone forever wonder
just what the hell it is.

The World Back Then

When I was young –
and that was long ago –
the world was very different –
you should have seen it then.

The woods behind my house
had trees to climb
and birds that sang –
a world just full of wonder.

Blue skies and white clouds
overhead on clear sunny days
a creek with crystal water,
and hidden paths to wander.

Through those woods were
fields of corn and cows in pastures,
and farmers that waved from
high up on their tractors

Then someone turned the
water brown and skies to gray,
and even drove the farms
and honeybees away.

But it's OK, I know,
time marches on and
change must have its place
in this grand growing world.

Blue skies and clouds,
trees and crystal creeks
and birds and bees and farms
will always be there – on my iPad.

I'd Still Be Me

We all dream of
winning the lottery.
But if I did, I know
I'd still be me.

Me in my Ferrari
Me in my Lear jet
Me on my Benetti yacht
Me with my Picasso
Me wearing my Rolex
Me on the beach –
     on my private island
Just me, still being me.

Windmill

It seems a shame
to be a man collecting dust.
The windmill turns no more.
I am becoming rust.

Blink

It seems, in the blink of an eye,
we morphed from
building snowmen and
trails in the woods
to whatever we are now.

How did we, suddenly one day,
forget how to play
and how far imagination
could take us, and get to
wherever we are now?

How did the dreams, back then,
of Superman and cowboys
fighting the black hats
become this, become
whoever we are now?

Old Boxes

The attic is filled with dozens of old boxes,
stored with bits and pieces of old lives
in different cities, at younger ages, and
when some of this stuff seemed important.
Clean out is a few laughs and a lot of
Why did I keep this?

So much of no-sense value –
pieces for the scrapbook of the mind.
Photographs, before digital cameras,
loose, never albumized,
a college calendar from 1969,
an old conch shell with a hole
from some forgotten movie scene.
Army uniforms (much too small now),
Programs from a Broadway play,
ticket stubs for Bob Seger,
the list and piles are endless.

There should have been at box or two
of old baseball cards or comic books,
worth at least a million dollars.
But, sadly, there were not.
And so, the attic now is empty.
Nothing remains of the old pieces of younger me.
Nothing remains except old dust.

Extreme Differences

I have been in the arena
and heard the crowds roar
and been in solitude
and heard the silence more.

I have been the hero
and heard the ovations
and been the loser
and heard castigations.

I've been famous
and heard adulation
and been forgotten
and heard denigration.

I've been in love
and heard birds sing
and been out of love
and heard nothing.

I prefer the arena.
And hero.
And famous.
And especially love.

Once Upon a Time, I Used to Be Me

Once upon a time
I used to be me.
I knew what I could do,
and what I wanted to be.

No one asked if I had dreams
so I began to think I shouldn't,
and the life I wanted to have
began to look like one I couldn't.

So I began that grow-up trip,
cutting away pieces of me,
a little at a time, so slowly
I never even noticed.

Every day, another piece
discarded in the far-back mind,
replaced with the new pieces
everyone said I had to find

And then one day, suddenly
I'd passed through the grow-up route
and now I am this collection of pieces.
I don't give a damn about.

But I can still remember,
once upon a time,
when I used to be me.

It's You

It's you –
it's always been you

Along the way
all the others
were just experiments
that failed
while I looked for you.

I wondered
if I would find you,
wondered if
and when.

And now –
it's you.
Finally.

Ugophobia

I have an incredibly
severe case of
ugophobia.

The fear that
you go away.

Cowboy Dreams

We were small once,
my dreams and me.
A cowboy riding
his broomstick pony,

The dreams got larger
as I grew older,
but never as real or as fun
as that broomstick soldier.

Younger Me

Younger Me
never thought about
Older Me
and what I might be.

Younger Me
never thought about
the path from youth
to Older Me

Now Older Me
thinks too often about
Younger Me
and what I failed to be.

Maid-Rite

Sometimes we all need
a trip back to some place
with some piece of a memory space
that still remains.

So every year I go back in time
to the Maid-Rite drive thru line,
see the gum wall again and
eat more steamed cheeseburgers.

It's still not an apartment building
or grocery parking lot,
or even worse, an empty bulldozed
memory-only spot.

Sometimes we all need
a trip back to
a piece of us
that still remains.

Life's Melted Candles

My life is a trip
through a candle shop,
lighting one for each
dream, where I stop.

So many have just
burned out, dropping
wax on the table, turning
cold and just stopping.

A few still flicker,
but all grow shorter
and dimmer as time
and dreams grow colder.

I light one more –
there still is a chance,
for at least enough light
for life's last dance.

Old Man

An old man is chasing me –
I look over my shoulder
and see him getting closer.

But the sun is still shining,
And I am still running
away from the old man.

The night darkness is near,
The roads are harder to see.
I hear him gaining on me.

An old man is chasing me –
I look in my mirror
and see him when I shave.

The Old is winning –
Old always wins.
But I am fighting hard.

My Expectations

I have learned along the way,
to be more complacent
about my expectations
of those in my life.
The less I expect,
the less I am hurt
by those who do not
live up to the expectations
they know nothing about.

Me, the Old House

One day I'll leave this run-down house
that's stood so many years along the river.
It's been dressed in many colors, and
repaired so many times,
it no longer resembles
what it started out to be.

The roof is fading and
the window glass is fogged.
The floors all creak and
the plumbing leaks a little.
It makes noises in the night,
and the lights are getting dimmer,
with old smells and lots of scratches
and joints with lots of patches.

When one day, the shutters close,
the lights go dark, and the house collapses,
I'll cross that river to God's town.
And no one will remember
I was just a house by the river,
once new, now fallen down.

Mr. Ok Sometimes

I'll never be Mr. Wonderful,
charming, attentive, thoughtful,
although I do feed the birds.

I'll never be Mr. Amazing,
the one to buy a dozen roses randomly,
but I can fix a faucet.

But sometimes when
my guard slips down,
I can do something sweet.

Just don't expect it often –
That's why they call me
Mr. OK Sometimes.

Without You

Without you I'd just be a falling star
with no tail lighting the sky,
a tiny dot in black heavens

Without you I'd be a southbound train
with no smokestack trail
rising in the sky behind me

Without you I'd have no music,
be still-dancing all alone
to no favorite song.

Without you I'd have no remembries
filling cracks and crevices in my mind
and holes in my heart.

Without you, I'd be no me.

Hourglass

The sand in an hourglass
pours through the bore
to the floor below,
stopping for no one.

There is continually
More past and less future.
More mistakes, more regrets,
Fewer maybes and what-ifs.
More we-did-it's.
More sorrows, and
more great moments,

More knowing
it's been a helluva ride.

Minstrel

I am the minstrel of my life,
just as you are yours.
Each of us creates a song
that only we can sing.

And when it ends,
when our last bell rings,
we are each a musical
no one else can ever sing.

One Morning

One morning
the day will start without me.
And the sun will rise, and the birds will sing,
the winds will blow, and the clouds will flow
through the day without me.

And that day
the night will start without me.
And the sun will set, and the stars will shine
and the moon will pass across the sky
through the night without me.

It won't be the end.
There will be another day,
and time to remember
life isn't about this moment,
but all the moments with you
that led to this last one.

And that day
I hope that you all know
how lucky I was that
the sun and birds and wind and clouds,
the night and moon and stars and God
shared all of you with me.

Smile for Me

Do not put me in some
hole in the ground,
and cry there for me.

Spread my ashes to the winds,
so I can spend eternity
mixed in drops of rain,
dew on a rose petal,
nurturing a farmer's corn,
feeling the sunshine,
reflecting the moon shine,
making rainbows
and mud puddles.

Do not cry for me in some hole –
Smile for me and the glory of our days.

On the Day I Die

We write eulogies for the dead,
who do not hear the words said.
So eulogies are not for those gone,
but rather for those remaining.

I don't want a eulogy of
tears and pains to be my final day.
I've lived a good and lucky life,
so when we make that final drive…

Roll all the windows down,
crack a beer, yell and laugh,
crank up the music
and sing along –
to Buffett and Chesney,
and Beatles and Stapleton.
Sing Celebration and Sweet Caroline
And Five O'Clock Somewhere
and My Life by Pam Rose.

Find a park, or field, or pond,
toss my ashes to the winds, and play
The Shires and Jimmy Allen
On The Day I Die.

My Book

Once upon a time
I came into this world to live a while.
And then one day to die.

And in that live-a-while time,
to have the chance to travel
the skyways, highways, and alleys
of a singular life full of the
skyway joys of simple moments
and highways searching for me,
and alleys hiding from my pains and errors.

Everyone will always have
some regrets, but I think
most of mine have been
the right ones.
And if not, I've erased those
chapters from my life.

My clothes aren't always right,
my words aren't always kind,
and sometimes my facts are probably
more what I want them to be
than reality.
But in the end,
it's been
My Book.

The End

Everything always works out in the end.
Eventually all the problems are solved
or become irrelevant.

Until that happens,
it's not The End.